The Art of Overcoming Obstacles

Introduction to Parkour: What Is It and How Did It Start?

Parkour is a physical discipline that involves moving from one point to another in the most efficient and graceful way possible, using only the human body and the environment as tools. The goal of parkour is not to perform stunts or tricks for the sake of entertainment, but to overcome obstacles, both physical and mental, and to express oneself creatively through movement.

The origins of parkour can be traced back to France in the late 1980s, when a group of young men began to explore the urban landscape of their city, using their bodies to navigate through the obstacles that they encountered. This group, known as the Yamakasi, developed a unique training methodology that emphasized natural movement, functional fitness, and mental discipline. The Yamakasi saw parkour not only as a way to stay fit and have fun, but also as a way to challenge themselves and to explore the limits of their physical and mental abilities.

The term "parkour" itself was coined by David Belle, one of the original members of the Yamakasi, who is often considered the founder of the modern parkour movement. Belle was born in 1973 in Fécamp, a small town in Normandy, and grew up in Lisses, a suburb of Paris. Belle's father was a veteran of the French military, and he taught his son the importance of physical fitness, discipline, and self-defense. Belle's mother was a gymnast, and she encouraged her son to develop his natural agility and grace.

Belle's childhood experiences in Lisses, where he and his friends would play games of tag and chase through the streets and rooftops, were the inspiration for his later development of parkour. Belle saw the urban environment as a playground and a challenge, and he began to train himself and others in the art of efficient movement. Belle's philosophy was simple: to move from one point to another as quickly, safely, and smoothly as possible, using only the body and the mind.

Over time, Belle's parkour practice began to attract attention from other young people in France, who were drawn to the physical and mental challenges of the discipline. Belle and his colleagues began to teach parkour to others, and they founded the first parkour group, called "ADD" (Art Du Déplacement), in the late 1990s. The ADD philosophy was based on the principles of natural movement, functional fitness, and mental discipline, and it quickly spread throughout France and beyond.

Today, parkour is practiced by thousands of people all over the world, who see it as a way to stay fit, to explore their creativity, and to connect with others who share their passion. Parkour has also inspired other disciplines, such as freerunning, which emphasizes acrobatics and artistic expression, and military obstacle course training, which emphasizes strength and endurance.

In summary, parkour is a physical discipline that involves moving through the environment in the most efficient and graceful way possible, using only the human body and the mind. Parkour originated in France in the late 1980s, and was developed by a group of young men who saw the urban environment as a playground and a challenge. The founder of modern parkour is David Belle, who coined the term and developed the philosophy of natural movement, functional fitness, and mental discipline. Today, parkour is practiced by thousands of people all over the world, who see it as a way to stay fit, to explore their creativity, and to connect with others who share their passion.

The History of Parkour: From France to the World

Parkour is a relatively young discipline, but its history is rich and complex. In this chapter, we will explore the origins and evolution of parkour, from its humble beginnings in France to its global popularity today.

The Roots of Parkour in France

The roots of parkour can be traced back to the suburbs of Paris, where a group of young men began to explore the urban environment in a new and unconventional way. These young men, who called themselves the Yamakasi, were inspired by a variety of influences, including martial arts, gymnastics, and urban culture.

The Yamakasi saw the city as a playground, and they began to use their bodies to navigate through the obstacles that they encountered. They developed a unique training methodology that emphasized natural movement, functional fitness, and mental discipline. This methodology, which they called Art Du Déplacement (ADD), became the foundation of modern parkour.

The Rise of David Belle

One of the most influential figures in the development of parkour is David Belle, who is often considered the founder of the modern parkour movement. Belle was born in Fécamp, a small town in Normandy, in 1973, and grew up in Lisses, a suburb of Paris.

Belle's childhood experiences in Lisses, where he and his friends would play games of tag and chase through the streets and rooftops, were the inspiration for his later development of parkour. Belle saw the urban environment as a playground and a challenge, and he began to train himself and others in the art of efficient movement.

Over time, Belle's parkour practice began to attract attention from other young people in France, who were drawn to the physical and mental challenges of the discipline. Belle and his colleagues began to teach parkour to others, and they founded the first parkour group, called ADD, in the late 1990s.

The Spread of Parkour Worldwide

As parkour began to gain popularity in France, it also began to attract attention from other parts of the world. In the early 2000s, parkour videos began to circulate on the internet, and the discipline quickly gained a global following.

Parkour communities began to emerge in countries such as the United Kingdom, the United States, and Australia, and parkour practitioners began to share their knowledge and techniques online. This led to the development of a global parkour culture, which emphasized the values of community, creativity, and self-expression.

Today, parkour is practiced in countries all over the world, and it has inspired a wide range of disciplines and movements, including freerunning, military obstacle course training, and urban exploration. Parkour has also become a popular subject in popular culture, with numerous films,

TV shows, and video games featuring parkour-inspired action sequences.

In summary, parkour originated in the suburbs of Paris in the late 1980s, and was developed by a group of young men who saw the urban environment as a playground and a challenge. The founder of modern parkour is David Belle, who developed the philosophy of natural movement, functional fitness, and mental discipline. Parkour quickly spread to other parts of the world, thanks to the internet and a global parkour culture, and today it is practiced in countries all over the world.

The Founding Fathers of Parkour: Who They Are and What They Did

Parkour is a discipline that was developed by a group of young men in France in the late 1980s and early 1990s. These men, who are often referred to as the "founding fathers" of parkour, were instrumental in creating the philosophy, techniques, and culture that define parkour today.

In this chapter, we will explore the lives and contributions of the founding fathers of parkour, and how their ideas and practices continue to influence the discipline today.

David Belle

David Belle is widely considered to be the founder of modern parkour. Born in Fécamp, France in 1973, Belle grew up in Lisses, a suburb of Paris. Belle's father was a veteran of the French military, and he taught his son the importance of physical fitness, discipline, and self-defense. Belle's mother was a gymnast, and she encouraged her son to develop his natural agility and grace.

Belle's childhood experiences in Lisses, where he and his friends would play games of tag and chase through the streets and rooftops, were the inspiration for his later development of parkour. Belle saw the urban environment as a playground and a challenge, and he began to train himself and others in the art of efficient movement.

Belle's philosophy was based on the principles of natural movement, functional fitness, and mental discipline. He believed that the body was designed to move in a certain way, and that by training the body to move naturally, people could overcome obstacles and challenges in their environment.

Sebastien Foucan

Sebastien Foucan is another key figure in the development of parkour. Born in 1974 in Paris, Foucan was a member of the Yamakasi group, which was founded by Belle and his colleagues in the late 1990s.

Foucan's contribution to parkour was the development of freerunning, a discipline that emphasizes acrobatics and artistic expression. While parkour is focused on efficient movement, freerunning allows for more creative and dynamic movement, including flips, spins, and other acrobatic maneuvers.

Foucan also emphasized the importance of mental discipline in parkour and freerunning, and he developed a philosophy that emphasized self-awareness, introspection, and personal growth.

Other Founding Fathers of Parkour

In addition to Belle and Foucan, there were other key figures in the development of parkour. These include:

- Chau Belle Dinh: A member of the Yamakasi group and a pioneer of parkour in France.
- Yann Hnautra: A member of the Yamakasi group and a key figure in the development of the ADD training methodology.

- Laurent Piemontesi: A member of the Yamakasi group and a parkour instructor who has trained many of the top parkour athletes in the world.

Together, these men developed the philosophy, techniques, and culture that define parkour today. They saw parkour not only as a way to stay fit and have fun, but also as a way to challenge themselves and to explore the limits of their physical and mental abilities.

In summary, the founding fathers of parkour were a group of young men in France in the late 1980s and early 1990s, who developed the philosophy, techniques, and culture that define parkour today. The most prominent of these men are David Belle and Sebastien Foucan, but there were also other key figures who contributed to the development of the discipline. Together, these men saw parkour as a way to challenge themselves and to explore the limits of their physical and mental abilities.

The Philosophy of Parkour: Mindset, Ethics, and Values

Parkour is not just a physical discipline, but also a philosophy that emphasizes a particular mindset, ethics, and values. In this chapter, we will explore the philosophy of parkour, and how it influences the way that parkour practitioners approach their training and their lives.

Mindset: The Way of the Traceur

Parkour practitioners, also known as traceurs, approach movement in a unique way. They see the urban environment as a playground, and they use their bodies to navigate through it in the most efficient and creative way possible.

The mindset of the traceur is one of constant curiosity and exploration. They see every obstacle as a challenge, and they are always looking for new ways to push themselves and to improve their skills. They also value creativity and self-expression, and they see parkour as a way to express themselves through movement.

In addition, the mindset of the traceur emphasizes mental discipline and focus. Parkour requires a high level of concentration and awareness, and traceurs must learn to control their fear and their emotions in order to perform at their best.

Ethics: The Code of the Traceur

Parkour also has a code of ethics that emphasizes respect, responsibility, and safety. The code of the traceur is based on the principles of mutual respect, self-improvement, and non-competition.

Traceurs are taught to respect their environment, other people, and themselves. They are also encouraged to take responsibility for their own safety and to avoid putting themselves or others at risk.

In addition, traceurs are encouraged to focus on their own progress and self-improvement, rather than comparing themselves to others. They also avoid competition, as parkour is not a sport but a discipline that is practiced for personal growth and expression.

Values: The Spirit of Parkour

The values of parkour are rooted in the discipline's philosophy and ethics. Parkour values creativity, self-expression, and innovation, and encourages practitioners to find their own unique style and approach to movement.

Parkour also values community and social connection. Parkour communities are tight-knit and supportive, and practitioners often train and explore together. This sense of community and belonging is a key part of the parkour experience.

Finally, parkour values perseverance and resilience. Parkour is a challenging discipline that requires a high level of physical and mental fitness. Practitioners must be willing to push themselves to their limits and to overcome obstacles and setbacks in order to achieve their goals.

In summary, the philosophy of parkour emphasizes a particular mindset, ethics, and values. The mindset of the traceur is one of curiosity, exploration, and mental discipline. The ethics of parkour are based on respect, responsibility, and safety, and discourage competition. The values of parkour include creativity, community, and perseverance. Together, these elements make up the spirit of parkour, which is focused on personal growth, self-expression, and exploration.

The Training Methodology of Parkour: Principles, Techniques, and Drills

Parkour is a discipline that requires a high level of physical and mental fitness, as well as a specific set of skills and techniques. In this chapter, we will explore the training methodology of parkour, including its principles, techniques, and drills.

Principles of Parkour Training

The training methodology of parkour is based on several key principles. These include:

1. Natural Movement: Parkour emphasizes the use of natural movements that mimic the way the body is designed to move. These movements include running, jumping, climbing, balancing, and crawling.
2. Efficiency: The goal of parkour is to move through the environment in the most efficient way possible. This means using the least amount of energy and effort to overcome obstacles and reach a destination.
3. Safety: Parkour practitioners prioritize safety above all else. They train to avoid injury, and they always assess the risks before attempting any movement.
4. Progression: Parkour training is based on progression. Practitioners start with basic movements and gradually increase the difficulty as they become more skilled and experienced.

Techniques of Parkour Training

Parkour training involves a variety of techniques that are designed to improve physical fitness, develop specific skills, and prepare for real-world challenges. These techniques include:

1. Conditioning: Parkour training includes a variety of conditioning exercises, such as running, jumping, climbing, and strength training. These exercises are designed to improve overall fitness and prepare the body for the demands of parkour.
2. Precision: Precision is a technique that involves landing and balancing on narrow surfaces, such as rails or walls. This technique helps to develop balance, control, and coordination.
3. Vaults: Vaults are movements that involve jumping over or onto an obstacle while using the hands to support the body. Vaults help to improve speed, power, and coordination.
4. Wall Runs: Wall runs involve running up a vertical surface, such as a wall or a building. This technique helps to develop leg strength and explosive power.

Drills for Parkour Training

Parkour training also involves a variety of drills that are designed to develop specific skills and techniques. These drills include:

1. Quadrupedal Movement: Quadrupedal movement involves moving on all fours, like a monkey or a lizard. This drill helps to develop agility, balance, and coordination.

2. Rail Precision: Rail precision involves jumping from one rail to another, using the feet to grip and control the movement. This drill helps to develop precision, control, and coordination.

3. Wall Climb-Ups: Wall climb-ups involve climbing up a vertical surface using the hands and feet. This drill helps to develop upper body strength and coordination.

4. Cat Leaps: Cat leaps involve jumping from one surface to another while grabbing onto a ledge or bar. This drill helps to develop explosive power and coordination.

In summary, the training methodology of parkour is based on a set of principles, techniques, and drills that are designed to develop physical fitness, specific skills, and mental discipline. The principles of parkour training include natural movement, efficiency, safety, and progression. The techniques of parkour training include conditioning, precision, vaults, and wall runs. The drills for parkour training include quadrupedal movement, rail precision, wall climb-ups, and cat leaps. Together, these elements make up the training methodology of parkour, which is focused on preparing practitioners to overcome real-world obstacles with grace, efficiency, and creativity.

The Physical Benefits of Parkour: Strength, Endurance, Flexibility, and Coordination

Parkour is a physically demanding discipline that requires a high level of fitness and athleticism. In this chapter, we will explore the physical benefits of parkour, including its effects on strength, endurance, flexibility, and coordination.

Strength

Parkour training is designed to improve overall strength and power. The discipline requires a lot of upper body and core strength, as well as lower body strength for jumping, running, and climbing. Parkour training includes a variety of exercises and drills that target different muscle groups, such as push-ups, pull-ups, squats, and lunges. Parkour also requires a lot of explosive power, which is developed through drills such as wall runs, cat leaps, and precision jumps. Explosive power is essential for overcoming obstacles quickly and efficiently.

Endurance

Parkour requires a lot of cardiovascular endurance, as practitioners often run, jump, and climb for extended periods of time. Parkour training includes a variety of conditioning exercises, such as running, jumping, and climbing, which improve overall endurance. Parkour also improves anaerobic endurance, which is the ability to perform high-intensity movements for short periods of time. This is essential for movements such as vaults, which require bursts of speed and power.

Flexibility

Parkour requires a lot of flexibility, especially in the hips, shoulders, and back. Flexibility is essential for movements such as vaults, precision jumps, and wall runs, which require a wide range of motion.

Parkour training includes a variety of stretching exercises, such as hip openers, shoulder stretches, and spinal twists, which improve overall flexibility. Stretching is also important for preventing injury and improving recovery time.

Coordination

Parkour requires a lot of coordination, as practitioners must be able to move their bodies in a fluid and efficient way. Parkour training includes a variety of drills that improve coordination, such as rail precision, quadrupedal movement, and cat leaps.

Coordination is also essential for movements such as vaults, which require precise timing and control. By improving coordination, parkour practitioners are able to move more efficiently and with greater grace.

In summary, parkour has a variety of physical benefits, including improvements in strength, endurance, flexibility, and coordination. Parkour training is designed to improve overall fitness and athleticism, and includes a variety of exercises and drills that target different muscle groups and energy systems. By improving physical fitness, parkour practitioners are better able to navigate their environment with grace, efficiency, and creativity.

The Mental Benefits of Parkour: Confidence, Focus, Resilience, and Creativity

Parkour is not just a physical discipline, but also a mental one. In addition to improving physical fitness, parkour also has a variety of mental benefits. In this chapter, we will explore the mental benefits of parkour, including its effects on confidence, focus, resilience, and creativity.

Confidence

Parkour requires a lot of confidence, as practitioners must be willing to take risks and push themselves out of their comfort zones. Through parkour training, practitioners learn to overcome fear and to trust in their abilities.

Parkour also teaches practitioners to believe in themselves and to have confidence in their decision-making. Practitioners learn to assess risks and to make decisions quickly and confidently, which translates to other areas of their lives.

Focus

Parkour requires a high level of focus and concentration. Practitioners must be able to stay present in the moment and to block out distractions in order to perform at their best. Through parkour training, practitioners learn to improve their focus and concentration. They develop mental discipline and learn to control their thoughts and emotions, which allows them to stay focused on their goals.

Resilience

Parkour is a challenging discipline that requires a lot of perseverance and resilience. Practitioners must be able to overcome obstacles and setbacks in order to achieve their goals.

Through parkour training, practitioners learn to develop mental toughness and resilience. They learn to push through pain and discomfort, and to keep going even when things get tough.

Creativity

Parkour is a discipline that encourages creativity and self-expression. Practitioners are encouraged to find their own unique style and approach to movement, and to be creative in their training and exploration.

Through parkour training, practitioners learn to think outside the box and to find creative solutions to challenges. They develop a sense of curiosity and exploration, which allows them to approach their environment with a sense of wonder and creativity.

In summary, parkour has a variety of mental benefits, including improvements in confidence, focus, resilience, and creativity. Parkour training teaches practitioners to overcome fear, improve their focus and concentration, develop mental toughness and resilience, and to be creative in their approach to movement. By improving mental fitness, parkour practitioners are better able to navigate their environment with confidence, creativity, and resilience.

The Cultural Impact of Parkour: Media, Art, and Community

Parkour has had a significant cultural impact, inspiring a variety of artistic expressions and building tight-knit communities around the world. In this chapter, we will explore the cultural impact of parkour, including its influence on media, art, and community.

Media

Parkour has been featured in a variety of media, including films, television shows, commercials, and music videos. The discipline's unique movements and style have made it a popular subject for filmmakers and advertisers alike.

One of the most well-known examples of parkour in media is the 2006 film "District B13," which features parkour practitioner David Belle. The film helped to popularize parkour around the world and inspired a new generation of practitioners.

Parkour has also been featured in video games, such as "Assassin's Creed," which incorporates parkour movements into its gameplay mechanics. The popularity of parkour in video games has helped to increase its visibility and inspire new practitioners.

Art

Parkour has also had an impact on the art world, inspiring a variety of artistic expressions. Parkour practitioners often use their movements as a form of self-expression, and the discipline's unique style has inspired artists in a variety of mediums.

For example, street artists often incorporate parkour movements into their art, creating murals and installations that depict parkour practitioners in motion. Parkour photography is also a popular art form, capturing the beauty and grace of the discipline's movements.

Community

One of the most significant impacts of parkour is the sense of community that it fosters. Parkour communities are tight-knit and supportive, with practitioners often training and exploring together.

Parkour communities also organize events, such as jams and competitions, which bring practitioners together from around the world. These events help to build a sense of camaraderie and belonging within the parkour community.

Parkour communities also often have a strong focus on social and environmental activism. Many practitioners see parkour as a way to connect with their environment and to promote sustainability and social justice.

In summary, parkour has had a significant cultural impact, inspiring a variety of artistic expressions and building tight-knit communities around the world. The discipline has been featured in a variety of media, including films, video games, and commercials, and has inspired artists in a variety of mediums. Parkour communities are known for their sense of camaraderie and social and environmental activism, and have helped to build a strong and supportive global community of practitioners.

The Globalization of Parkour: How It Spread and Adapted to Different Cultures

Parkour originated in France in the 1990s and has since spread around the world, adapting to different cultures and environments. In this chapter, we will explore the globalization of parkour, including how it spread and adapted to different cultures.

Spread of Parkour

The spread of parkour can be attributed to several factors. One of the main drivers of parkour's global popularity is the internet. Parkour videos and tutorials are widely available online, making it easy for anyone to learn and practice the discipline.

Parkour has also been featured in a variety of media, including films, television shows, and commercials. These appearances have helped to increase parkour's visibility and inspire new practitioners.

Parkour communities have also played a significant role in its global spread. Parkour practitioners often travel and train with other practitioners around the world, sharing their knowledge and expertise.

Adaptation to Different Cultures

Parkour has adapted to different cultures and environments around the world. Practitioners in different regions have incorporated their own unique styles and approaches to the discipline, making it more diverse and inclusive.

For example, in Japan, parkour has been influenced by the art of Budo, a Japanese martial art that emphasizes discipline and mental focus. Japanese parkour practitioners often focus on precision and control, using their movements as a form of meditation.

In Brazil, parkour has been adapted to the urban landscape, with practitioners using their movements to navigate the crowded city streets. Brazilian parkour practitioners often incorporate dance and capoeira movements into their practice, creating a unique fusion of disciplines.

In the United States, parkour has been adapted to the American landscape, with practitioners incorporating movements such as wall flips and tricking into their practice. American parkour communities also often have a strong focus on social and environmental activism.

In summary, parkour has spread around the world, adapting to different cultures and environments. The internet, media, and parkour communities have all played a role in its global popularity. Parkour has been adapted to different cultures and regions, making it more diverse and inclusive. The adaptation of parkour to different cultures has created a unique and global community of practitioners, united by their love of movement and exploration.

Parkour in Europe: France, United Kingdom, Spain, Germany, and Beyond

Parkour originated in France and has since spread throughout Europe, inspiring a variety of practitioners and communities. In this chapter, we will explore the history and current state of parkour in Europe, focusing on France, United Kingdom, Spain, Germany, and beyond.

France

France is considered the birthplace of parkour, and the discipline has a strong presence in the country. The founders of parkour, David Belle and Sébastien Foucan, both hail from France.

Parkour communities in France are known for their focus on discipline and mental toughness. French practitioners often incorporate running and climbing into their practice, using the urban landscape as their playground.

The French parkour community is also known for its social and environmental activism, with many practitioners advocating for sustainable living and social justice.

United Kingdom

The United Kingdom has a vibrant parkour community, with practitioners often organizing events and competitions. The discipline is also widely taught in schools and fitness centers.

The British parkour community is known for its creativity and innovation. British practitioners often incorporate gymnastics and freerunning movements into their practice, creating a unique fusion of disciplines.

Parkour has also been used as a tool for social and community development in the United Kingdom. The charity organization, Parkour Generations, uses parkour to engage young people and promote positive social change.

Spain

Spain has a growing parkour community, with practitioners often incorporating acrobatics and martial arts movements into their practice. Spanish parkour communities are known for their creativity and fluidity of movement.

The Spanish parkour community is also known for its focus on inclusivity and diversity. Many Spanish parkour communities have programs and initiatives to promote gender and racial equality within the discipline.

Germany

Germany has a strong and organized parkour community, with many practitioners organizing events and competitions. German parkour communities often focus on efficiency and precision of movement.

The German parkour community is also known for its emphasis on safety and injury prevention. Many German practitioners incorporate physical therapy and injury prevention techniques into their training.

Beyond

Parkour has also spread throughout other European countries, such as Italy, Poland, and Russia. These countries have developed their own unique styles and approaches to the discipline, making it more diverse and inclusive.

In summary, parkour has a strong presence in Europe, with thriving communities in France, United Kingdom, Spain, Germany, and beyond. Each country has its own unique style and approach to the discipline, creating a diverse and inclusive global community of practitioners. Parkour has also been used as a tool for social and community development, promoting positive change and social justice.

Parkour in North America: USA, Canada, Mexico, and Brazil

Parkour has spread throughout North America, inspiring a variety of practitioners and communities. In this chapter, we will explore the history and current state of parkour in North America, focusing on the United States, Canada, Mexico, and Brazil.

United States

The United States has a thriving parkour community, with practitioners organizing events and competitions across the country. Parkour has also been incorporated into fitness programs and schools.

American parkour communities often incorporate gymnastics and tricking movements into their practice, creating a unique fusion of disciplines. The American parkour community is also known for its focus on creativity and self-expression.

Many American parkour communities also have a strong focus on social and environmental activism, advocating for sustainable living and social justice.

Canada

Canada has a growing parkour community, with practitioners organizing events and competitions across the country. Parkour has also been incorporated into physical education programs in schools.

Canadian parkour communities often incorporate skateboarding and snowboarding movements into their practice, creating a unique fusion of disciplines. The Canadian parkour community is also known for its focus on inclusivity and diversity.

Mexixo

Mexico has a growing parkour community, with practitioners often using the urban landscape as their playground. Mexican parkour communities often incorporate dance and acrobatics movements into their practice, creating a unique fusion of disciplines.

Mexican parkour communities are also known for their focus on creativity and self-expression. Many Mexican practitioners see parkour as a form of art and self-expression.

Brazil

Brazil has a thriving parkour community, with practitioners often incorporating capoeira and dance movements into their practice. Brazilian parkour communities are known for their fluidity and grace of movement.

The Brazilian parkour community is also known for its focus on inclusivity and diversity. Many Brazilian practitioners see parkour as a way to promote social and racial equality.

In summary, parkour has spread throughout North America, with thriving communities in the United States, Canada, Mexico, and Brazil. Each country has its own unique style and approach to the discipline, creating a diverse and inclusive global community of practitioners. Parkour has also been used as a tool for social and community development, promoting positive change and social justice.

Parkour in Asia: Japan, China, South Korea, and Malaysia

Parkour has spread throughout Asia, inspiring a variety of practitioners and communities. In this chapter, we will explore the history and current state of parkour in Asia, focusing on Japan, China, South Korea, and Malaysia.

Japan

Japan has a strong and growing parkour community, with practitioners often incorporating martial arts and Budo movements into their practice. Japanese parkour communities are known for their precision and control of movement.

Japanese parkour practitioners often see the discipline as a form of meditation and focus on mental discipline and control. The Japanese parkour community is also known for its emphasis on safety and injury prevention.

China

China has a growing parkour community, with practitioners often incorporating traditional Chinese martial arts movements into their practice. Chinese parkour communities are known for their fluidity and grace of movement.

Chinese parkour practitioners often see the discipline as a form of self-expression and creativity. The Chinese parkour community is also known for its focus on discipline and mental toughness.

South Korea

South Korea has a thriving parkour community, with practitioners often incorporating acrobatics and dance movements into their practice. South Korean parkour communities are known for their energy and creativity.

South Korean parkour practitioners often see the discipline as a form of art and self-expression. The South Korean parkour community is also known for its focus on community building and social activism.

Malaysia

Malaysia has a growing parkour community, with practitioners often using the urban landscape as their playground. Malaysian parkour communities often incorporate traditional Malay martial arts movements into their practice.

Malaysian parkour practitioners often see the discipline as a way to connect with their environment and promote sustainability. The Malaysian parkour community is also known for its focus on inclusivity and diversity.

In summary, parkour has spread throughout Asia, with thriving communities in Japan, China, South Korea, and Malaysia. Each country has its own unique style and approach to the discipline, creating a diverse and inclusive global community of practitioners. Parkour has also been used as a tool for social and community development, promoting positive change and social justice.

Parkour in Africa: Senegal, Morocco, South Africa, and Egypt

Parkour has spread throughout Africa, inspiring a variety of practitioners and communities. In this chapter, we will explore the history and current state of parkour in Africa, focusing on Senegal, Morocco, South Africa, and Egypt.

Senegal

Senegal is considered one of the birthplaces of parkour in Africa, and the discipline has a strong presence in the country. Senegalese parkour communities often incorporate traditional Senegalese wrestling movements into their practice.

The Senegalese parkour community is known for its focus on discipline and mental toughness. Many practitioners also see parkour as a way to promote social and racial equality.

Morocco

Morocco has a growing parkour community, with practitioners often using the urban landscape as their playground. Moroccan parkour communities often incorporate traditional Moroccan movements into their practice.

The Moroccan parkour community is known for its focus on creativity and self-expression. Many Moroccan practitioners see parkour as a form of art and self-expression.

South Africa

South Africa has a thriving parkour community, with practitioners often incorporating breakdance and hip-hop movements into their practice. South African parkour communities are known for their energy and creativity.

The South African parkour community is also known for its focus on social and environmental activism. Many practitioners use parkour as a way to connect with their environment and promote sustainability.

Egypt

Egypt has a growing parkour community, with practitioners often using the ancient architecture of the country as their playground. Egyptian parkour communities often incorporate traditional Egyptian movements into their practice.

The Egyptian parkour community is known for its focus on discipline and mental toughness. Many practitioners also see parkour as a way to connect with their culture and heritage.

In summary, parkour has spread throughout Africa, with thriving communities in Senegal, Morocco, South Africa, and Egypt. Each country has its own unique style and approach to the discipline, creating a diverse and inclusive global community of practitioners. Parkour has also been used as a tool for social and community development, promoting positive change and social justice.

Parkour in Oceania: Australia, New Zealand, and Fiji

Parkour has spread throughout Oceania, inspiring a variety of practitioners and communities. In this chapter, we will explore the history and current state of parkour in Oceania, focusing on Australia, New Zealand, and Fiji.

Australia

Australia has a thriving parkour community, with practitioners often incorporating surfing and skateboarding movements into their practice. Australian parkour communities are known for their energy and creativity.

The Australian parkour community is also known for its focus on inclusivity and diversity. Many practitioners use parkour as a way to promote gender and racial equality within the discipline.

New Zealand

New Zealand has a growing parkour community, with practitioners often using the natural landscape of the country as their playground. New Zealand parkour communities often incorporate traditional Maori movements into their practice.

The New Zealand parkour community is known for its focus on discipline and mental toughness. Many practitioners also see parkour as a way to connect with their culture and heritage.

Fiji

Fiji has a small but growing parkour community, with practitioners often using the natural beauty of the country as their playground. Fijian parkour communities often incorporate traditional Fijian movements into their practice.

The Fijian parkour community is known for its focus on community building and social activism. Many practitioners use parkour as a way to connect with their community and promote positive change.

In summary, parkour has spread throughout Oceania, with thriving communities in Australia, New Zealand, and Fiji. Each country has its own unique style and approach to the discipline, creating a diverse and inclusive global community of practitioners. Parkour has also been used as a tool for social and community development, promoting positive change and social justice.

Parkour and Urbanism: How the City Shapes the Practice and Vice Versa

Parkour is intimately connected to the urban environment, with practitioners using the city as their playground. In this chapter, we will explore the relationship between parkour and urbanism, and how the city shapes the practice and vice versa.

The City as Playground

Parkour practitioners see the city as a playground, using the urban landscape to explore movement possibilities and express their creativity. The built environment provides an endless array of challenges and obstacles, from walls and railings to stairs and rooftops.

Parkour also challenges the traditional use of urban space, encouraging practitioners to see the city in a new way. The discipline promotes a sense of ownership and empowerment, with practitioners reclaiming public space and using it for their own purposes.

The City as Partner

The city is not just a backdrop for parkour, but an active participant in the practice. The built environment shapes the movements and techniques that practitioners use, influencing the evolution of the discipline.

Different cities also have their own unique styles and approaches to parkour. Practitioners in Tokyo, for example, often use the city's dense urban environment to develop precision and control of movement. In contrast, practitioners in London often incorporate freerunning and tricking movements into their practice, taking advantage of the city's wide-open spaces.

Urbanism as Inspiration

Parkour has also been an inspiration for urban designers and architects, who have sought to create more "parkour-friendly" cities. Some designers have incorporated parkour-specific features, such as railings and walls, into their designs, while others have created more flexible and adaptable urban spaces that allow for a greater variety of movement.

Urbanism as Challenge

At the same time, parkour practitioners have also challenged the traditional models of urban design and planning. The discipline has highlighted the importance of public space and the need for more inclusive and accessible cities. Parkour practitioners have also been involved in urban activism, advocating for sustainable living and social justice. The discipline has the potential to create positive change in the urban environment, promoting a more equitable and resilient future.

In summary, parkour and urbanism are deeply connected, with the city shaping the practice and vice versa. Parkour practitioners see the city as a playground, using the urban landscape to explore movement possibilities and express their creativity. At the same time, parkour has also been an inspiration and challenge for urban designers and activists, promoting a more inclusive and sustainable urban future.

Parkour and Risk: Safety, Injury Prevention, and Legal Issues

Parkour is a high-risk activity that involves jumping, climbing, and vaulting over obstacles in urban environments. In this chapter, we will explore the importance of safety, injury prevention, and legal issues in parkour.

Safety

Safety is paramount in parkour, as the discipline involves a high risk of injury. Practitioners should always warm up and stretch before beginning their practice, and should wear appropriate clothing and protective gear.

It is also important for practitioners to develop a strong foundation of technique and skill before attempting more advanced movements. Practitioners should also practice in safe and controlled environments, and should avoid practicing in areas with uneven surfaces, loose debris, or other hazards.

Injury Prevention

Injury prevention is a key aspect of parkour practice. Practitioners should focus on developing strength, flexibility, and coordination through regular conditioning and training.

Practitioners should also listen to their bodies and avoid pushing themselves beyond their limits. It is important to rest and recover after a practice session, and to seek medical attention if any injuries occur.

Legal Issues

Parkour is often viewed as a high-risk and dangerous activity, and there are legal issues that practitioners should be aware of. In some cases, parkour may be seen as a form of trespassing, as practitioners may be using public or private property without permission.

It is important for practitioners to respect the laws and regulations of the areas where they practice, and to obtain any necessary permissions or permits before practicing in public spaces.

Conclusion

Parkour is a high-risk activity that requires practitioners to prioritize safety, injury prevention, and legal issues. Practitioners should focus on developing a strong foundation of technique and skill, and should practice in safe and controlled environments.

At the same time, parkour has the potential to promote positive change and social justice, and has been used as a tool for community building and development. By prioritizing safety and responsible practice, parkour can continue to be a positive and inspiring discipline for practitioners around the world.

Parkour and Competition: Events, Rules, and Formats

Parkour is primarily a non-competitive discipline, with practitioners focused on personal development and self-expression. However, in recent years, competitive events have emerged, creating new opportunities for practitioners to showcase their skills and compete against others. In this chapter, we will explore the world of parkour competition, including events, rules, and formats.

Events

Parkour competitions can take many forms, from individual freestyle events to team-based relay races. Some competitions may focus on specific aspects of parkour, such as speed or technique, while others may be more freestyle and open-ended.

One of the most prominent parkour competitions is the Red Bull Art of Motion, which features a series of freestyle runs in which athletes are judged on their creativity, difficulty, and execution. Other notable events include the World Chase Tag Championships, which is a team-based event featuring a tag-style format, and the Speed Project, which challenges athletes to complete a parkour course as quickly as possible.

Rules

Parkour competitions typically have a set of rules and guidelines that athletes must follow. These rules may include restrictions on certain movements, such as flips or spins, and may require athletes to complete specific obstacles or challenges within a certain time frame.

Judges evaluate each athlete's performance based on a variety of criteria, including technical skill, creativity, difficulty, and execution. Athletes are often given a set amount of time to complete their runs, with deductions for any mistakes or falls.

Formats

Parkour competition formats can vary widely, from individual freestyle runs to team-based relay races. Some competitions may also incorporate elements of other sports or disciplines, such as gymnastics or dance.

Freestyle competitions allow athletes to showcase their creativity and personal style, while speed and obstacle-based competitions challenge athletes to complete courses as quickly and efficiently as possible. Relay races and team-based events emphasize collaboration and strategy, requiring athletes to work together to overcome obstacles and complete challenges.

Conclusion

Parkour competition has emerged as a new and exciting facet of the discipline, creating opportunities for athletes to showcase their skills and compete against others. While competition is not the primary focus of parkour, it has the potential to inspire and motivate practitioners, and to push the boundaries of the discipline.

As the world of parkour competition continues to evolve, it is important for athletes and organizers to prioritize safety, respect, and sportsmanship. By embracing these values and staying true to the spirit of parkour, competition can continue to be a positive and inspiring aspect of the discipline.

Parkour and Education: How It Can Be Used for Teaching and Learning

Parkour is not just a physical discipline, but also a philosophy and a mindset. As such, it has the potential to be a powerful tool for teaching and learning in a variety of contexts. In this chapter, we will explore how parkour can be used in education, including physical education, youth development, and social and emotional learning.

Physical Education

Parkour can be a valuable addition to physical education curricula, providing a fun and engaging way for students to develop strength, endurance, and coordination. By incorporating parkour movements and techniques into physical education classes, teachers can encourage students to explore their physical capabilities and challenge themselves in new ways.

Parkour can also promote a sense of self-efficacy and confidence in students, as they learn to overcome obstacles and take risks in a safe and controlled environment.

Youth Development

Parkour can be a powerful tool for youth development, helping young people to build resilience, discipline, and social skills. By emphasizing the values of respect, responsibility, and collaboration, parkour can create a positive and supportive community for young people to grow and learn.

Parkour can also promote a sense of ownership and empowerment in young people, as they learn to take control of their environment and their lives. By providing a space for creativity and self-expression, parkour can help young people to develop their identities and explore their passions.

Social and Emotional Learning

Parkour can also be used to teach social and emotional learning (SEL) skills, such as self-awareness, self-regulation, and empathy. By emphasizing the importance of self-care and self-reflection, parkour can help practitioners to develop a strong sense of self and a positive self-image.

Parkour can also promote empathy and understanding, as practitioners learn to navigate their environment and interact with others in a respectful and supportive way. By emphasizing the importance of communication and collaboration, parkour can help practitioners to develop strong relationships and a sense of community.

Conclusion

Parkour has the potential to be a powerful tool for teaching and learning, in a variety of contexts. By emphasizing the values of respect, responsibility, and collaboration, parkour can create a positive and supportive environment for personal growth and development. Whether in physical education, youth development, or social and emotional learning, parkour can help individuals to develop their physical, social, and emotional capabilities, and to reach their full potential.

Parkour and Social Justice: Diversity, Inclusion, and Empowerment

Parkour is not just a physical discipline, but also a philosophy and a mindset that promotes inclusivity, empowerment, and social justice. In this chapter, we will explore how parkour can be used as a tool for promoting diversity, inclusion, and social justice.

Diversity

Parkour promotes diversity by welcoming individuals of all backgrounds, abilities, and identities to participate in the discipline. Parkour communities around the world are made up of individuals from diverse racial, ethnic, and socio-economic backgrounds.

Parkour also challenges traditional gender roles and expectations, promoting a more inclusive and equitable approach to movement and athleticism. By celebrating diversity, parkour creates a supportive and welcoming environment for practitioners to explore their physical and creative potential.

Inclusion

Parkour promotes inclusion by creating a supportive and collaborative community that welcomes individuals of all levels and abilities. Parkour communities often organize training sessions and events that are open to all, regardless of skill level or experience.

Parkour also promotes a growth mindset, emphasizing the importance of effort and progress over innate ability. By focusing on the process of learning and development, parkour encourages practitioners to support and learn from one another, rather than competing against each other.

Empowerment

Parkour promotes empowerment by giving individuals the tools and skills to navigate their environment and overcome obstacles in their lives. Parkour practitioners often describe feeling a sense of agency and control over their environment, as they learn to use the urban landscape to their advantage.

Parkour also promotes a sense of self-efficacy and confidence, as practitioners learn to take risks and challenge themselves in a safe and controlled environment. By emphasizing the importance of perseverance and determination, parkour can help individuals to develop a strong sense of self and a positive self-image.

Social Justice

Parkour has the potential to promote social justice by challenging traditional power structures and promoting a more equitable and inclusive society. Parkour communities often organize events and initiatives that support social justice causes, such as environmental sustainability and community development.

Parkour can also be used as a tool for urban activism, promoting the importance of public space and the need for more inclusive and accessible cities. By empowering individuals to take control of their environment and their lives, parkour can help to promote positive change and social justice.

Conclusion

Parkour promotes diversity, inclusion, and empowerment, and has the potential to be a powerful tool for social justice. By creating a supportive and welcoming community that celebrates diversity and promotes inclusion, parkour can help individuals to develop their physical, social, and emotional capabilities, and to reach their full potential. Whether through community events, urban activism, or personal development, parkour can be a positive and inspiring force for social change.

Parkour and Entrepreneurship: How to Build a Career in Parkour

Parkour is a discipline that offers a wide range of opportunities for entrepreneurship and career development. From coaching and training to event production and content creation, there are many ways to turn a passion for parkour into a successful career. In this chapter, we will explore how to build a career in parkour, including some tips and strategies for success.

Identify Your Skills and Passion

The first step in building a career in parkour is to identify your skills and passion. Are you passionate about coaching and teaching others? Or do you have a talent for event production and organization? Do you have a knack for creating engaging content and building a social media following? By identifying your strengths and interests, you can begin to explore the different career paths available in parkour.

Get Certified and Educated

To build a successful career in parkour, it is important to have the necessary certifications and education. Many parkour organizations offer coaching and instructor certification programs, as well as courses in event production, marketing, and business management. By investing in your education and professional development, you can gain the skills and knowledge necessary to succeed in the industry.

Build Your Network

Networking is a key part of building a successful career in parkour. Attend events and conferences, join parkour communities and organizations, and connect with other professionals in the industry. By building relationships and networking with others, you can gain valuable insights and opportunities, as well as access to potential clients and partners.

Create Your Brand and Market Yourself

Creating a strong personal brand and marketing yourself effectively is essential in building a career in parkour. Develop a unique style and approach to coaching or training, create engaging and compelling content, and use social media and other marketing channels to build your brand and reach your audience. By building a strong and recognizable brand, you can differentiate yourself from competitors and attract potential clients and partners.

Diversify Your Income Streams

To build a sustainable career in parkour, it is important to diversify your income streams. Consider offering coaching, training, and event production services, as well as creating and monetizing content through social media and other platforms. By diversifying your income streams, you can create a more stable and reliable source of income, as well as build multiple revenue streams that support each other.

Conclusion

Building a career in parkour requires passion, dedication, and a willingness to take risks and explore new opportunities. By identifying your skills and passion, investing in your education and professional development, building your network, creating a strong personal brand, and diversifying your income streams, you can turn your love for parkour into a successful and fulfilling career.

Parkour and Future: Trends, Innovations, and Challenges

Parkour has come a long way since its origins in the streets of France. Today, it is a global phenomenon with a passionate and growing community of practitioners and fans around the world. In this chapter, we will explore the trends, innovations, and challenges facing parkour in the future.

Trends

One of the biggest trends in parkour is the increasing professionalization and commercialization of the discipline. As parkour becomes more popular and mainstream, there is a growing demand for high-quality coaching, training, and event production services. This trend is creating new opportunities for entrepreneurship and career development in the industry.

Another trend is the increasing diversity and inclusivity of parkour communities around the world. As parkour becomes more accessible and welcoming to individuals of all backgrounds and identities, it is helping to promote a more inclusive and equitable society.

Innovations

Parkour is a discipline that is constantly evolving and adapting to new environments and challenges. One of the biggest innovations in recent years has been the development of new training and coaching techniques, including online coaching and remote learning.

Another innovation is the use of technology to create new and innovative ways to experience and engage with parkour. This includes the use of virtual reality and augmented reality to simulate parkour environments and movements, as well as the use of drones and other devices to capture and share parkour performances and events.

Challenges

Despite its growth and success, parkour faces several challenges in the future. One of the biggest challenges is the need to balance commercialization and professionalization with the values and ethics of the discipline. As parkour becomes more mainstream and commercialized, there is a risk of losing the grassroots and community-focused nature of the discipline. Another challenge is the need to address safety and legal issues related to parkour. As parkour continues to grow and attract new practitioners, there is a need for clear guidelines and regulations to ensure the safety of practitioners and others in the community.

Conclusion

Parkour has a bright and exciting future, with many trends and innovations driving its growth and success. By embracing diversity and inclusivity, and promoting entrepreneurship and innovation, parkour can continue to grow and evolve in the years to come. However, it is important to address the challenges facing the discipline, including the need to balance commercialization and community-focused values, and the need for clear guidelines and regulations related to safety and legal issues. By addressing these challenges, parkour can continue to thrive and inspire individuals around the world.

Conclusion: The Legacy of Parkour and Its Message to the World

Parkour is more than just a physical discipline. It is a philosophy and a mindset that promotes resilience, creativity, and empowerment. Throughout its history, parkour has inspired individuals around the world to overcome obstacles and challenges in their lives, and to pursue their goals with passion and determination. In this final chapter, we will reflect on the legacy of parkour and its message to the world.

The Legacy of Parkour

The legacy of parkour is a legacy of resilience and innovation. From its origins in the streets of France to its global popularity today, parkour has inspired individuals to push beyond their limits and to explore the boundaries of what is possible. Parkour has also contributed to the development of new training and coaching techniques, as well as new innovations in technology and media.

Another legacy of parkour is its message of inclusivity and diversity. Parkour has created a global community of individuals from diverse backgrounds, abilities, and identities, who share a passion for movement, creativity, and exploration. Through this community, parkour has helped to promote a more inclusive and equitable society, where everyone has the opportunity to pursue their dreams and reach their full potential.

The Message of Parkour

The message of parkour is a message of empowerment and resilience. Parkour teaches individuals to navigate their environment with confidence and creativity, and to overcome obstacles and challenges with perseverance and determination. Parkour also promotes a growth mindset, emphasizing the importance of effort and progress over innate ability, and encouraging individuals to support and learn from one another.

Parkour also promotes a sense of social responsibility, encouraging individuals to use their skills and talents to contribute to their communities and to promote positive change in the world. Whether through urban activism, social justice initiatives, or personal development, parkour inspires individuals to use their passion and creativity to make a difference in the world.

Conclusion

Parkour is more than just a sport or a hobby. It is a philosophy and a mindset that has inspired individuals around the world to pursue their dreams, overcome obstacles, and make a difference in the world. Through its legacy of resilience, innovation, inclusivity, and social responsibility, parkour has left an indelible mark on the world, and will continue to inspire and empower individuals for generations to come.

Thank you for reading this book on parkour. We hope that it has been informative, engaging, and inspiring. As a language model, it is our goal to provide you with accurate and useful information to help you better understand the world around you.

If you enjoyed this book and found it helpful, please consider leaving a positive review. Your feedback will help us improve our services and continue to create informative and engaging content for our readers.

Manufactured by Amazon.ca
Acheson, AB

15828185R00035